Adventures in Chocolate

Hand-Made Truffles at Geoffroi

Geoffrey & Joan Hazzan

ADVENTURES IN CHOCOLATE

Geoffrey & Joan Hazzan

photographs by Dan Ringquist

ISBN: 978-1-963565-23-2 (Paperback)

Library of Congress Control Number: 2024911117

Printed in the United States of America

Published by

info@thequippyquill.com
(302) 295-2278

Other books by Joan Vernikos (Hazzan)

THE G-CONNECTION: HARNESS GRAVITY AND REVERSE AGING
iUniverse, 2004 with Robin S Hosie and Republished by Quippy Quill, 2024

STRESS FITNESS for SENIORS
Thirdage Books, 2009

SITTING KILLS, MOVING HEALS
Quill Driver Books, 2011

To our GEOFFROI devotees

" *P*eople will forget what you said, people will forget what you did, but people will never forget how you made them feel."

---Maya Angelou

ACKNOWLEDGMENTS

Special thanks to Jim, Werner and Martin for their regular encouragement and assistance. We extend our appreciation to Gregory R. Copley, AM, for his inspired editorial advice and support.

CONTENTS

Geoffrey's Catalyst

*C*old War's Wintry blustering had been underway for so long that it was part of normal life for us all. But then, in 1983, the pace of it intensified. British Prime Minister Margaret Thatcher and US President Ronald Reagan piled the pressure on a faltering Soviet Union. Little did they consider that they had begun moving me to a fateful decision. They put Joan and me onto the path of our Adventure in Chocolate.

An embargo was placed on the import from the USSR of raw materials for the plastics industry: polyethylene, PVC granules and the like. Thus, absent competitively priced raw materials to make British plastics, I lost my job of 27 years, selling and marketing in the plastics industry in the United Kingdom and Europe.

Joan and I decided to use this setback as an opportunity to try our hands at something new. But what? An upscale bed-and-breakfast hotel with a grass tennis court and small pool was one option. A wine-bar was another.

Perhaps I had been dreaming, because upon waking up one morning I suggested opening a chocolate shop. I saw a twinkle in Joan's eye but the proviso was that we make the chocolates rather than just buy and sell them. We both had a sweet tooth but no manufacturing experience. Quietly, I thought this would at best last a few months and we would then simply buy in Belgian, French or Swiss chocolates.

This chocolate memoir selectively chronicles the extraordinary six-year adventure of our Winchmore Hill's GEOFFROI. The unusual spelling we gave the enterprise was to differentiate it from the numerous hair-stylists and florists in Greater London's thick telephone directory. It also had a certain aura with a chic Anglo-Gallic ring about it. Our house colors were an elegant Bordeaux Green and Gold.

We deliberately avoided the use of machinery and concentrated on hand-made, hand-rolled fresh cream truffles with a short shelf life. Joan's pharmacological skills were at once put to the test. Our modest kitchen in North London became the scene of frenzied activity for three weeks. My own onerous role was to take charge of Quality Control as I eagerly tasted the product while watching the BBC news at 9.00 pm. It was a very tough assignment. "All were yummy" I declared. My total appreciation landed me in very hot water for being unable to rate and decide which of Joan's 23 assorted formulations we should offer our customers. We finally settled on six truffles.

Starting with a variety of recipes culled and adapted from newspapers and magazines, most were conjured up and soon modified along the way. Customer feedback, likes and dislikes, were later the source of inspiration. The origin of each recipe has a story. This book, *Adventures in Chocolate*, is interspersed with these real life vignettes. The recipes are original and proprietary and published for the first time though the products have been enjoyed by our dinner party guests these last few years.

One of the pleasures of running a niche business was the ability to make decisions on the spot without having to refer to others. I could accept or summarily turn down bulk orders according to my judgment.

I rejoiced at no longer having to drive 30,000 miles a year for my job. Meanwhile, Joan was on extended leave of absence from NASA's Ames Research Center in California. We lived in Southgate close to the business and kept our overheads low. After lengthy persuasion the local health inspector, a butterfly buff, agreed the neighborhood would have no cause to complain of noxious chocolate fumes! Our cottage industry was first able to start up in two rooms overlooking a small garden of a Winchmore Hill back alley.

Tales of GEOFFROI

The word chocolate was invented by the Spanish from a combination of the word *cacahuatl*, that is Aztec for bitter water, and the Mayan word for hot water — *chocol haa to make chocolatl.*

No fanfare attended the opening of our "Mom-and-Pop" enterprise in 1983. We just began paying rent and started work. We invited some friends along and initially found it difficult to take their money! We soon got over that. We never advertised. We relied on the curious and on word of mouth and the aroma of chocolate that greeted them.

A trickle of customers began, within days, to beat a path to our shop. The local newspaper wrote: "You would never suspect that inside a small house in Winchmore Hill, a NASA scientist is working on a secret formula which could greatly affect the lifestyle of many people throughout the world ... the weight watchers dream — the sugar free truffle!" It would, in fact, be a couple of years before we experimented with sugar-free truffles.

GEOFFROI *The Shop Drawing Keith West, 1984*

Not unexpectedly youngsters, brought up on *Willy Wonka and the Chocolate Factory* soon dropped in to see in wide-eyed wonder what we were up to. Joan was particularly understanding and patient with them. Nicholas Chrisostomou and Stuart Thomas from the local private Keble School were soon regulars. Nicholas, with dark long eye-lashes and curly hair, had a singing part in the Chariots of Fire film.

He then became a member of a children's singing and dancing troupe of all nationalities and backgrounds, Kids International, which was an instant hit on BBC Television. In later years, Nicholas ran a popular London nightclub and has already written an autobiography!

The Challenge of Making Truffles

Neither of us had the slightest idea how to make chocolate truffles not to mention work with chocolate. Yes, we had entertained friends to dinner and made the odd cake recipe, but there our experience ended. Joan naively thought that it would be no different than making — those were the days when you actually made — pills and suppositories at the local chemist. She is also the kind of person who does not faithfully follow instructions but always adapts and improvises. This sometimes makes for unexpected delights or disasters.

Our First Christmas

Our first Christmas came within three months of our opening. It was Christmas Eve and the shop was emptied of everything we could make except for one box waiting to be picked up. Exhausted and elated we celebrated by dancing to the radio music. Because of the bright lights in the shop, we could not see who might be coming but we were plainly visible to those outside. Soon we saw a line of smiling faces outside the window.

Mixing Science and Chocolate

An unlikely episode occurred one Friday lunch-time. Professor Mary Mycek, Joan's long-standing friend from the New Jersey Medical School, happened to be staying with us. She was in London to attend the International Pharmacological Congress. Next day we took her to

GEOFFROI's, had her don a house-apron with the responsible task of rubber stamping small brown paper carrier bags in a corner of the shop.

Meanwhile, a satellite conference was held in Cambridge ahead of the Congress. After it was over, another friend, Glen van Loon, an endocrinology professor from the University of Kentucky, an avowed chocoholic, and some colleagues caught the stopping train to Winchmore Hill village. Included in this group was a local Englishman on a post-doctoral fellowship at Stanford University in California. He categorically assured Glen there was no chocolate-maker in his home village. Glen knew better having tasted Joan's products in California. 6 ft. 6 in. tall and wholly clad in baby-blue shirt, shorts, socks and sneakers he strode confidently into the sleepy Barclays corner bank and in a deliberately loud voice asked where GEOFFROI, the wonderful chocolate shop, was located?

After being directed to the back alley, Glen introduced his group. First, there was a lady from the National Institutes of Health (NIH) who was studying the effect of hormones on how the brain metabolizes barbiturate hypnotics. Joan, scooping and rolling truffles from a large bowl of rum truffle mix, asked if she knew Mary Mycek? No, she did not, but was, of course, familiar with her work. Joan pointed in Mary's direction who inclined her head and smiled back. A lively conversation followed. Next, the Englishman from Stanford was asked about his field? Neuroendocrinology. Which department? Psychiatry. With whom did he work? Dr Jack Barchas.

By now, the young man could hardly conceal his impatience at the temerity of the shop-keeper's questioning while stirring the chocolate truffle mixture. Joan could not resist retorting: "Oh, I helped get him started." Yet another visitor, who was Glen's post graduate, had what seemed a marked Egyptian accent. With pride he declared that he had studied at the School of Pharmacy, University of Alexandria — *Joan's alma mater* — and was all but speechless when she countered: "You will, of course, know Dean Mottawa."

Incongruous scenes such as this became the norm at GEOFFROI. We clearly did not conform to the stereotypical chocolatier.

The BBC's Michael Simpson was also an early and curious visitor. He directed plays on radio and television and, a little tongue-in-cheek, tried to provoke us. He asked if we ever quarreled — he was looking for suitable material — and was disappointed to find we seldom did. "A pity. Your chocolate shop would have had the makings of a good soap opera."

Chocolate

We sought, tasted and tested every source of chocolate. Most readers know that chocolate comes from roasting and extracting the cocoa beans of a cocoa tree. Many are now familiar with the history of how chocolate made its way into the western world through the Spanish Conquistadors. They discovered and picked up the habit of the joys of drinking chocolate from the Central and South American Mayans who drank the extracted cocoa liquor unsweetened. Despite its bitterness it was a favorite for its stimulant properties due mostly to theobromine, a relative of caffeine.

History of Chocolate. French Commemorative Stamps, 2009.

It was in Europe that sugar or milk was added to the dark cocoa liquor. The remaining white cocoa butter was used for medicinal purposes as lip balm or to make suppositories. Alternately, it was blended with milk and flavored with vanilla to produce what is now called white chocolate.

Chocolate is not a single ingredient but a composite of active ingredients such as theobromine, and mostly consists of a combination of fats that give it its particular texture and characteristics. Chocolate, not unlike wine, therefore differs considerably depending on its source, soil or climate which varies from year to year. It also differs depending on its method of processing, handling and storage.

The best chocolate melts at body temperature. In other words, it melts in the mouth at a rate that allows full appreciation of its flavor. The melting point of chocolate is determined by its relative composition of different fats which also can vary from one batch to another. Although attempts have been made to make synthetic chocolate any novice can tell the real thing. It is this varied composition in fats that make it so difficult to imitate and unpredictable to work with.

It was apparent that cocoa beans from the Ivory Coast produced the kind of chocolate we liked best. France's Valrhôna and Caxton's, a British manufacturer no longer in business, were the best sources for dark chocolate. We used white Belgian Callebaut.

But milk chocolate presented a dilemma. Belgian, Swiss and French varieties all seemed bland to us. Finally, we found what we were seeking in Caxton's almost on our doorstep. It had that distinctive smoky caramel flavor that distinguished the original Cadbury bars we had grown up with. The foreman at Caxton's related how a worker burned a vat of chocolate. He took it off the fire but it was so hot he dropped it on the floor. As he tried to clean up, he put his chocolate-covered finger in his mouth. So was born English milk chocolate with that very different, smoky flavor quite unlike any other.

English or American Ingredients?

The recipes in this book have had to be adapted from the original English recipes to cater for American ingredients as well; cream and butter, in particular, produced different consistencies. Do not assume that all white chocolate is created equal either. Since 2004, white chocolate needs to be at least 20 percent (by weight) cocoa butter, at least 14 percent total milk solids and less than 55 percent sweeteners such as sugar. Therefore the content of cocoa butter can vary greatly. The less cocoa butter, the more soupy was the truffle mixture. It was safer to stick with Belgian Callebaut.

Both UK and US recipes are provided. If you live elsewhere do not be surprised if the consistency turns out different. The percentage of fat in cream varies a great deal and the higher it is the smoother your product. The quality of the unsalted butter used can also vary extensively. That is because there can be quite a bit of water in butter as well as residual salt which also vary with the origin of the butter. The safest way around that is to melt the butter and then let it set in the fridge. You may then pour off the excess water from the pure butter.

All the original recipes were based on British ingredients of 28 years ago. We assumed the same would be true globally only to find out the hard way that this was not necessarily so. The hard way meant that the correct smooth consistency for scooping the truffle mixture was not achieved. Playing around with the proportions of cream to butter to chocolate only distorted the smoothness and the flavor. Testing our English recipes in the USA we ate many a soupy, "gone wrong" batch — not good for one's waist but which friends and neighbors did not seem to mind. It was very frustrating. The results were inconsistent and not up to our standards. Making chocolates only on special occasions made solving these problems slow. Gradually, the reason became clear: fat.

Butter

All butter is not created equal. The answer came from a most unlikely source: Greek New Year's cookies. Last Christmas I decided to bake some traditional *kourabies: kourayebah* in the Middle East. These are something similar to Mexican wedding cookies but there the similarity ends. My friend Irene's are always superb, delicate, mouth-watering products. Her secret has been to melt and simmer for a few minutes sweet unsalted butter, allow it to cool and refrigerate till hard. Cut large chunks of the solid butter and scrape off any white froth from the top and bottom of the butter. Pour out any clear liquid which is surprisingly salty. I pat the chunks gently with paper towels to remove any trace of this liquid. I then whip the butter a little with an electric mixer until white and fluffy and store it covered and refrigerated. Known as clarification this process has been used since 1769 to remove impurities from butter. Clearly you end up with less butter than you started out with. The following American recipes are based on using clarified butter. Even if the label contents seem identical, it is amazing how different brands of butter vary in liquid, salt and the content of white froth and impurities. This pretreatment results in pure butter whatever its source and thereby standardizes the recipes.

Cream

Neither is all cream created equal. Fat content of heavy cream in the US is 8 percent. You may find 9 percent occasionally in specialty shops. In England double cream is 14 to 16 percent. Halving the amount of cream is not the answer. The solution is to simmer the cream down to half its volume. The proportion of fat is doubled by this process. Take care not to burn the lactose sugar in the cream, which imparts a caramel flavor unless so desired.

Hooking Customers

We made a point of winning customers over by offering generous tasters. All made appreciative noises yet we soon noticed there were two distinct types of chocolate eaters. The majority popped them like pills — feeding strawberries to a donkey — while the more discerning would gently bite into the truffle the better to savor. We nicknamed them "poppers" and "connoisseurs".

The Original Six

Joan was experimenting well before we opened the shop. She started reading recipes from magazines and cookbooks. Armed with bags of chocolate chips from California, she would at first test a recipe ready to be savored and evaluated after the evening news. As we sampled and settled on better sources of chocolate the products improved. This was not an easy process. Geoffrey had not yet acquired a fine chocolate palate. Nerves were frayed as the reality of our commitment set in. Our personal partnership and venture may well have ended there and then.

We finally settled on starting with six that provided variety in taste and appearance, a little bit for everyone we thought, with some dark, milk and white chocolate varieties: Grand Marnier dark, Grand Marnier white-coated and Rum for the dark chocolate purists, Cherry Kirsch for the milk chocolate, Mocha for the coffee and Amaretto for the nut lovers.

The Original Six

"Research tells us that 14 out of every 10 individuals like chocolate."

— *Sandra Boynton Chocolate : The Consuming Passion*

At first we made mostly dark or milk chocolate truffles: Rum, Grand Marnier coated in dark or white chocolate, Amaretto, Cherry Kirsch and Mocha. We used white chocolate, Amaretto, Cherry Kirsch and Mocha. We used real liqueurs and spirits only, not essences, and no preservatives, additives or extracts.

The Rum Truffle is the king of truffles. Probably the first ever made. Even those who claim not to care much for chocolate will recognize the name. Easy to make, but you need to go slowly. Because it is basic and designed to bring out the best in chocolate it can easily go wrong. What makes the difference? Do not rush. Use the most flavorful chocolate, the right balance of the purest unsalted butter, richest cream and the best dark rum you can find.

The texture of the perfect Rum Truffle must be luscious, smooth and melt exactly at the temperature of your mouth to allow you to fully savor the rich flavors as it gradually melts. None of our recipes have any added sugar. Sugar is used commercially to cover up the taste of poorer quality chocolate so the better the quality of chocolate, the less sugar is added. A touch of bitterness brings out the best in the chocolate flavor.

Dipping truffles 1984

Dipping truffles 1984

Many rum truffles are made of *ganache* — the name given to the mixture of equal parts of chocolate and cream. Though mostly used to decorate chocolate cakes, it is the foundation of all truffles and modified by adding butter, eggs, nuts, fruit, coffee, liqueurs and other flavorings. Our rum truffles contain some butter to give the mixture a smoother consistency.

Julia Child used coffee to flavor her rum truffle. We added a touch of grated orange peel. You can use grated fresh orange peel if you plan to eat the truffles right away. If you are a chocoholic, both are "to kill for!" Plain rum truffle made with the richest ingredients, without any other flavor is the king of them all.

Rum Truffles

Easy to make but should not be rushed. If well and gently blended these truffles will melt in the mouth.

Rum Truffles

Yield: 24 truffles

Ingredients

US recipe
6 oz bittersweet dark chocolate
4 oz heavy cream
4 oz clarified butter
2 tbsp dark rum

UK recipe
6 oz bittersweet dark chocolate
4 oz double cream
4 oz unsalted butter
2 tbsp dark rum

Optional Flavoring: ½ tsp dry orange peel powder or 1tsp fresh grated orange zest

Coating
Dutch cocoa powder (best quality unsweetened)

Directions
Break up chocolate into small pieces in an oven-proof glass measuring cup (16 oz)

Boil cream in a small heavy pan until reduced to 2oz. Remove from heat.

Add to broken chocolate, let sit 2 minutes and stir gently. Heat in a microwave oven for 5 seconds at a time stirring only until chocolate is just melted, no lumps are present. Since the mixture retains heat with microwaving be very careful after each heating not to overheat and scorch the mixture.

Gently whisk in butter till smooth. Add rum and stir to blend. Mixture should be cool, smooth and glossy. Cool to room temperature. Refrigerate for an hour or two until firm.

Roll into balls and store in air-tight containers in refrigerator for two weeks or freeze for longer periods.

Roll in cocoa, place in paper cups and allow to come to room temperature for an hour before serving. As with all chocolate truffles, they are best eaten fresh.

NB: Use good quality unsweetened cocoa. If there is any sugar in your cocoa, your rum truffles will "sweat" and lose their even powdered look. That is why drinking cocoa should not be used. Roll the powdered truffles lightly in the palm of your hand to get rid of extra cocoa. Too much cocoa dries out the truffle. Rolling too vigorously warms up the truffle and makes the cocoa covering uneven.

~~~~~

Truffles which pigs dig up are not meant to be smooth. When scooping and rolling, it is worth remembering that odd-shaped truffles bear an uncanny resemblance to the sniffed black ones from the French fields of Périgord!

Geoffrey and Hazel Martin, a delightful, gentle, elderly couple with a certain aura about them would visit the shop from time to time, always with a smile. He was the first to discover us one icy December afternoon when we were still in the back alley and soon brought his wife around. Geoffrey had been a life-long Toc H man accustomed to building a fairer society by working with communities to promote friendship and service. One son was headmaster of a famous boarding school whilst Roger was a senior diplomat at the Foreign Office. The great advantage of a small chocolate shop is the opportunity to get to know customers on an individual basis and usually having a chance to talk to them.

On this occasion Roger (now Sir Roger and a leading environmentalist) was ordering a box of truffles to take out to Harare in Zimbabwe, a hot posting in every way in the 1980s. I cautioned that truffles did not "travel" well and they would surely melt away in Southern Africa. "Don't worry, this is for my dinner party to-morrow night at the British High Commission and they'll all be eaten."

A few weeks later I received a letter asking for a favor. His mother's 80th birthday was coming up and he never knew what to give her as a present. He wanted to keep her morale up a little by arranging a regular supply, twice a month, for three months, and she could choose £5 worth each visit. A check for £30 was enclosed. I was touched and thrilled to be able to help with this special gift order.

Grand Marnier Truffles

This is a rich chocolate truffle center which we coated either in a dark or white chocolate shell. It is for the connoisseur to be eaten slowly and savored.

Grand Marnier Truffles. Black and White

Yield: 30 truffles

Ingredients

US Recipe
12 oz bittersweet Chocolate

UK Recipe
10 oz bittersweet chocolate

8 oz heavy cream	8 oz double cream
3 oz clarified butter	4 oz unsalted butter
3 tbsp Grand Marnier	3 tbsp Grand Marnier

Coating

1 lb tempered semisweet dark chocolate, or 1 lb tempered white chocolate

Directions

Boil the cream to reduce to 4oz. Pour over the chopped chocolate, add butter and stir until smooth. Stir in Grand Marnier. It should look smooth and glossy. Cool completely. Refrigerate covered overnight until firm. Scoop and shape into balls. Freeze uncovered on a tray until hard, about 2 hours or longer. Store frozen in covered container.

Tempering chocolate by hand

Chocolate must be tempered in order to obtain a smooth consistency and shiny surface. To achieve this you will need a thermometer in the range from 50°-150°F (10° - 60°C).

First chocolate must be melted by heating to 110°F (50°C), then cooled to 81°F (28°C) then re-warmed slightly to 86°- 90°F (30° -31°C) to make it easier to work with. It is then ready for molding or coating.

It is safest to work in no less than 1 lb batches. Less chocolate cannot be melted at an even temperature. Break chocolate into small pieces reserving about 4 oz finely grated for seeding. Melt in microwave for 30 seconds. Some use a double boiler but chocolate is very sensitive to moisture and it may lump and harden. Stir gently to mix. Return to microwave for another 30 seconds. Remove and continue to stir until completely melted and glossy avoiding air bubbles. Microwave heating continues after bowl is removed from oven. Be patient. Do not overheat beyond 110°F.

Add the reserved grated chocolate 1 tbsp at a time to seed the chocolate making sure it is completely melted before adding any more. You will know that by touching a drop on your lip. It should feel cool and the mixture will be thickening. Use a thermometer when you first start out. Now place chocolate over warm water to bring the temperature back between 86° to 90°F. You should always have some seeding chocolate left over.

If chocolates are coated while the coating is too warm they are likely to bloom. Blooming are the white streaks in the coating that result from coating that has not been tempered properly.

White chocolate is somewhat easier to temper but the same process applies.

Dip frozen truffle centers in tempered white or dark chocolate and decorate by touching the top of each truffle with a clean fork before coating sets completely.

~~~~~

With Joan commuting to California on a regular basis Thelma Bamford, a patron who lived by The Green, described her as a gypsy saying that all she lacked was a caravan; not too far off the truth. Flying in from San Francisco, Joan was chauffeured into town next day for an interview. The BBC radio's Mid-Week program after the 9.00 a.m. news gave us national publicity. Libby Purves, a skilled interviewer and journalist, had gathered together in the studio James Prior, a senior Tory politician, Robert Kilroy-Silk, a colorful Labor MP, Andreas Whittam Smith, founder editor of the new *Independent* newspaper, Roy Clark, a writer, a London busker (one-man band) and Joan. An hour's lively and humorous discussion followed.

Joan's two careers were deemed to be of bizarre diversity and she was asked the usual questions about astronauts suffering from vertigo and muscle-wasting. With regard to her studies at Ames, Purves asked: "Do you mean to say that a way to lose weight is to lie in bed for thirty days with your feet up eating chocolates?" "As long as you don't get out of bed at all even for natural reasons."

Asked if she had time to read American newspapers, Joan trod carefully. How did she switch her train of thought from scientific research and all things space to chocolates? "That's easy. I set my watch to the new time as soon as I board the plane. Then I start planning my next day's work."

Joan referred to Prior as a *"corporate guru"*. "I've never been called that before," was his response.

The program ended with the discordant drum beats and insistent puffing of a mouth organ as the busker plied his trade. Minutes later two customers pulled up by the curb to say they had been listening to Joan on their car radio.

Amaretto Truffles

Yield 30 truffles

Ingredients
9 oz bitter-sweet dark chocolate chopped
5 oz unsalted butter at room temperature
1 large egg
1¼ cups unblanched almonds ground fine
3 tbsp Amaretto

Coating
Tempered dark chocolate
Sliver blanched almonds for decoration

Directions
Break up and heat dark chocolate in medium-sized bowl in microwave, 30 seconds at time stirring in between until thoroughly melted. Do not overheat or scorch. Beat eggs and mix well with chocolate.

Blend in ground almonds. Ingredients will soon start to set. Add Amaretto and mix thoroughly.

Mixture will set naturally in 2-3 hours. Best if dipped and coated in dark tempered chocolate right away to avoid loss of flavor and drying.

Decorate with one almond sliver before coating has quite set. May be stored for up to a week in the refrigerator. NB. Do not freeze. There is no cream in this truffle so the recipe for US and UK is the same.

Simone Sekers is a well-known food writer in England who visited GEOFFROI. We were pleasantly surprised to find ourselves listed in her 1987 compilation of *Fine Food: a Directory of the best and where to find it in England, Wales and Scotland.* Sandwiched between Cooke's Eel and Pie shop and Mrs. Gill's Indian Kitchen in the London and South East section you will find Geoffroi's fresh cream truffles.

"A husband and wife team, the Hazzans began their truffle-making when Geoffrey was made redundant from his job in the plastics industry in 1983 – his wife still works as a pharmacologist. Not surprisingly, they felt that making hand-made truffles in small batches with the best ingredients, would provide a pleasant contrast to their careers. The truffles are wonderful – I fell for the Amaretto flavor covered in dark chocolate – and beautifully boxed in dark green, red and gold."

Cherry Kirsch Truffles

This truffle was extremely popular with anyone with German roots or who was fond of the taste of German Black Forest cake. It is the simplest to make and has no butter or added sugar.

Luscious Cherry Kirsch Truffles

Yield 30 truffles

Ingredients

US Recipe
8oz heavy whipping cream
(9% fat)
10 oz milk chocolate
2 tbsp Kirsch
¼ cup chopped candied cherries

UK Recipe
4 oz double cream
(14% fat)
9 oz milk chocolate
2 tbsp Kirsch
¼ cup chopped candied cherries

Coating
Finely ground whole roasted almonds.

Directions
Place cream in small pan over medium heat and boil till reduced to 4 oz making sure it does not spill over or scorch. Remove from heat. Add chocolate broken into small pieces. Cover and let stand 3 minutes. Stir until smooth and chocolate is blended.

Mix in Kirsch and finely chopped cherries. Mix with an electric mixer until well blended and lighter in color. Refrigerate overnight. Scoop into balls and roll lightly in ground almonds preferably just before serving. Eat and enjoy.

Eaten really fresh, they are divine. If refrigerated after being rolled in almond, they tend to dry. Mixture or scooped balls may be stored in a tight-covered container in the freezer.

~~~~~

Cherry Kirsch was our milk chocolate truffle staple. The quality of the milk chocolate is extremely important and, after Caxton's closed down, we used Belgian Callebaut. The candied cherries give it a sweetness that appealed to those with a sweeter tooth. Neither rum nor cherry kirsch truffles are chocolate-coated and therefore easier to make. It is best to eat them when really fresh.

Internationally acclaimed New Zealand mezzo-soprano Patricia Payne always asked for melt-in-the mouth Cherry Kirsch truffles which she dubbed "central heating." David Galloway, her distinguished lichenologist husband, preferred dark chocolate and would order a chunk of Callebaut as he came out of the station on his way home. One August day Patricia came to the shop and sang Happy Birthday – a moving operatic experience for Geoffrey.

Mocha Truffles

Yield: 30 truffles

Ingredients

8 oz hazelnut Praline*
3 to 6 tbsp instant espresso coffee** (as desired)
10 oz milk chocolate
8 oz heavy cream
1 tbsp Fra Angelico Hazelnut liqueur

Coating
White chocolate to coat.
Dark chocolate to decorate

Directions
Boil cream to reduce to 4ozs volume. Add coffee to hot cream. Soften milk chocolate by heating in microwave for 30 secs to 1 minute. Pour hot coffee cream over chocolate. Stir gently till all chocolate has melted. Cool to room temperature.

Mix in praline. Add liqueur to chocolate mixture. Beat with electric mixer till smooth.

Scoop and roll into balls. Cool in refrigerator.

Dip in white chocolate. Decorate with two dark chocolate lines.

Since these truffles contain no butter or eggs they can be stored refrigerated for longer periods than the others.

*Hazelnut praline can be found in specialty stores or from Amazon.com. Love'n Bake Hazelnut Praline comes in 11oz cans.

** Get good quality instant Espresso coffee such as Medalia D'Oro or Cafe Bustelo.

~~~~~

Returning from a hard-earned fleeting holiday in Israel, we were wandering around the duty-free shop as we awaited boarding instructions. Joan was quick to spot maestro Zubin Mehta, conductor of the Israel Philharmonic Orchestra, buying a complete set of China. From the *Chocolatier* magazine we knew of his passion for chocolates.

Geoffroi "I gather you are a chocoholic."

Mehta "I am President of the Chocoholics!"

Geoffroi "As a chocolate maker I would like to offer you a box to enjoy."

Mehta "To-morrow night at The Royal Opera House. Be sure to leave a card."

I worked feverishly on my return to London before delivering the chocolates back-stage but, alas, received no acknowledgement. To this day, I wonder if they 'fell off' a trolley on the way!

It was nevertheless the encouragement of the locals that was most rewarding. W.R. "Bill" Fletcher was one of those first regulars and introduced the rest of the Fletcher family to GEOFFROI. Son Keith and Marina Fletcher are established antiquarian booksellers. He tells the story that father Bill was counseled by his own father to think twice before entering the book trade "as the supply of good books will not last much longer."

We got to know the whole Fletcher clan who all had a marked penchant for luxury chocolates. They kindly introduced us to other antiquarian friends such as the Rota family, who then patronized GEOFFROI. Happily, our friendship has stood the test of time. When last we met in Much Hadham in 2001, we were presented with a rare edition of *Life On The Moon* in 1768 by Florentine artist Filippo Morghen as a blueprint for Joan's Space Tourism project. They recently sent us a French postal service set of stamps issued in 2009 that magnificently portrays the history of chocolate.

The Birth of the All-White Chocolate Truffle

$\mathcal{A}$lthough we coated some of the dark chocolate Grand Marnier truffles as well as the milk chocolate Mocha truffles in white chocolate, we had never made an all-white chocolate truffle. It transpired, as we discovered later, that neither had anyone else in Europe. *Leonidas Chocolates* in Belgium came close with a delicious *crème fraîche* center coated in white chocolate, but these were not, strictly speaking, truffles.

The Case of the Migraine Lady

One day, as was our custom, Joan offered a truffle to a customer. She looked at it in horror and declined. Joan was amazed at her atypical reaction. "I do not eat chocolate" the lady said. People who do not like chocolate are a rarity. "I get migraine headaches when I eat chocolate." This triggered Joan's pharmacological curiosity who promptly offered her one of our apricots. "Oh, no," she insisted.

White chocolate barely contains traces of cocoa liquor. It would have been surprising indeed if white chocolate would bring on her migraine headaches.

It turned out that fearing the dreaded migraine our customer had never tried white chocolate. Joan gave her a small chunk of white chocolate and suggested she try it when she got home. Next morning the lady returned beaming and ecstatically announced that no migraine had resulted. She went off with a bag of apricots to relish her new find. Joan then sat down to figure out how to make an all-white chocolate truffle.

White chocolate is essentially the cocoa butter extracted from cocoa beans separated out from the cocoa liquor. It is the ingredient found in your lip balm. Because it melts at body temperature it has been used for years to make suppositories! Blended with milk and sugar it comes either unflavored or faintly flavored with vanilla. It therefore lends itself readily to creative flavoring. We went to work.

Coffee was an obvious flavor for those who like their latte or cappuccino. Adding some Irish whiskey made an *Irish Coffee* in a bite. A chocolate coffee bean topped off the overall experience. We later made a Kahlua truffle for those who preferred a more subtle flavor.

From that point on we started asking visitors to GEOFFROI about their flavor preferences. This was a big help in deciding what to choose for other truffles – white, milk or dark – that we developed. Vodka Lime, Tia Maria, Malibu, Benedictine, The Dubliner and others all followed each with a story to match.

Cointreau Truffles

However, the very first all-white chocolate truffle we made for the migraine lady was the famous *Cointreau*, our all-time winning truffle.

The first all white chocolate Cointreau Truffle

Yield: 30 truffles

Ingredients

US recipe	**UK recipe**
16 oz white chocolate	14 oz white chocolate
7 oz heavy whipping cream	8 oz double cream
1oz clarified butter	2 oz unsalted butter
6 tsp grated orange zest	6 tsp grated orange zest
6 tbsp Cointreau liqueur	4-6 oz Cointreau liqueur
NB. US *recipe* boil	
cream to reduce to 3.5 oz	

Use dried (depending on quality) or fresh finely grated orange zest for best flavor.

Coating
Tempered white chocolate
Thin glacéd orange strip for decoration

Directions
Place cream, butter and peel in a small pan over low heat to melt and blend. When it starts to boil, turn off heat, cover and allow to rest for 2 minutes.

Add small pieces of chocolate all at once, cover and leave two to three more minutes. Stir gently until completely melted and blended. Allow to cool uncovered at room temperature giving it an occasional stir.

When at room temperature, add liqueur 1 tbsp at a time and gently blend in well.

Cover with cling film and refrigerate until of scooping consistency. This may take more than 24 hours.

Scoop mixture and quick-roll lightly in the palm of your hands. Place in tightly closed container and allow to freeze completely.

Dip frozen truffle centers in tempered white chocolate. Decorate with a strip of candied orange peel.

~~~~~

England's feisty cricket captain Mike Gatting – he appeared in 79 Tests and captained England to their last Ashes victory in Australia in 1986-87 – caused a stir when parking his marked Ford courtesy car immediately outside GEOFFROI. Suddenly, our shop was crowded! His wife and mother-in-law must have come in before because he immediately asked for and exhausted our stock of Cointreau truffles. They were "a nice little earner." On other occasions Gatting expressed concerns about his post-cricketing future. He was awarded an OBE in 1987 and is now an established commentator, journalist, and pundit of the game.

Tall, unassuming tennis star Jo Durie, the winner with Jeremy Bates of the Wimbledon Mixed Doubles in 1987 and the Australian Mixed Doubles in 1991, would sometimes drop in. She lived just down the road and trained locally. One of her Fischer tennis rackets proudly hangs on my sporting Wall of Honor.

One morning a slightly-built customer quietly walked in and seemed to know exactly what he wanted. As he was leaving there was something about him that I somehow recognized. Had he not once played soccer for the Republic of Ireland, I asked. "I still do!" It was Liam Brady, the elegant former Arsenal and Juventus midfielder, one of a select group ever to have scored a goal against Brazil. For the past 15 years, Brady has headed up the Arsenal F.C. youth academy for future stars.

Irish Coffee

This special Irish coffee truffle blends white chocolate coffee and Irish Whiskey into a special Irish cream with a chocolate coffee bean on top. It is preferable not to use chocolate covered coffee beans but a bean of chocolate that looks like a coffee bean. Make sure the chocolate coffee beans are made with good quality chocolate.

Finishing off Irish Coffee Truffles

Yield: 40 truffles

Ingredients

US recipe
16 oz white chocolate
2 oz heavy whipping cream
0.5 oz clarified butter
1 tsp instant espresso coffee
3 tbsp Rose's Irish Whiskey

UK recipe
16 oz white chocolate
8 oz double cream
2 oz unsalted butter
1tsp instant espresso
3 tbsp Rose's Irish Whiskey

Coating
Tempered white chocolate
Chocolate coffee beans for decoration

Directions
Boil cream in small pan to reduce to 1 oz. Add butter and coffee over low heat. When it starts to boil, turn off heat, stir to blend. Add all chocolate making sure cream mixture covers chocolate.

Allow to rest for 2-3 minutes. Stir gently just to melt and blend. Allow to cool uncovered stirring occasionally. When at room temperature, add whiskey one tbsp at a time making sure it blends well.

Cool in refrigerator until it sets hard preferably overnight. This is most important as the mix will otherwise be sticky and hard to handle. Scoop, roll lightly in your hands and allow to harden once more in the refrigerator. Store in air-tight container in the freezer. Will keep frozen for up to two weeks.

Dip frozen balls in tempered white chocolate and decorate with dark chocolate coffee bean before coating sets.

~~~~~

Phil Syme, a local customer friend, made it possible for Joan to be interviewed by Mark Smith on London's LBC radio. Since we did not advertise this was our big break. Needless to say she was eager to tell the world about our truffles. In particular, she described in great detail what the Irish Coffee truffle looked like.

Joan, "It's white chocolate and it's all white inside with a coffee bean on top and whisky-flavored."

Smith, "Right, I'll have a taste of that."

Joan, "This is just one. We make another one. We take suggestions from the customers…"

Smith, "That is delicious!"

Joan, "I'm glad you said that".

Smith, "That is. I'm not, as I said to you a few minutes ago before we came on air, I'm not really a chocolate fan, but that really is excellent."

The interview went splendidly. What Joan did not realize, however, was that in her excitement she forgot to mention the crucial information — the name of the shop and where it was located.

As if this promotional disaster were not enough, a week later we visited Fortnum and Mason's, the Queen's grocer, which we tended to do periodically to check on their chocolate display. There, before our disbelieving eyes, was something that looked identical to our Irish Coffee truffle. We bought one to see if it tasted like ours, but fortunately it did not. In fact, it was rather disappointing, but a partial relief to us.

By now we had moved around the block onto Station Road. The Victorian twin-gabled shop that had once served as the stationmaster's office was given a much-needed coat of paint. Mahogany shelves and cupboards were fitted. We brought in some antique furniture to add extra tone. To increase the volume of business, we supplemented the chocolate truffles with our own line of homemade preserves, chutneys, ice cream sauces along with freshly ground coffee beans, virgin olive or walnut oils and delicious sorbets that were a big hit in the summer.

APRIL ISSUE 18

SPACE AND FLAVOUR

For three months of the year Joan Hazzan is a space scientist at the NASA base in California. For the other nine months she makes luxury chocolates in North London. Felicity Green on one working woman's double life

from Working Woman UK, 1984

Felicity Green, the pioneering fashion journalist who played a major part in bringing both super model Twiggy as well as miniskirt and hot pants creator Mary Quant to public attention, came to Geoffroi to interview me about my living a dual role as a NASA scientist and chocolatier! Flatteringly, she wrote about my looking "a little like Ingrid Bergman in her prime … at the moment, Joan's mind is operating on two levels, a state well known to many women, albeit with less disparate fields of simultaneous endeavor." She quoted me as saying, "Here we're experimenting with diet truffles – not quite slimming, but less fattening – then back at NASA I'll be working on simulated weightlessness." Still in harness mentoring students at St Martin's, Felicity was awarded an OBE for services to journalism in 2012.

The buyer at Hobbs in Mayfair tipped us off that 70% of our annual turnover would come in between December 10th and Christmas. How very right she was. We worked an 18-hour day and although there was little elbow room took on help – Liza Lack, then a schoolgirl, is now a doctor. Advance orders were placed all to be fresh and ready for pick up on Christmas Eve. That was the challenge. Having everyone's truffles freshly made for the same day plus a very few extras for those who thought they could walk in without ordering and still not be disappointed. The only way was to work virtually around the clock. Sleep was something that had to be put off. You may wonder, as we did, how commercial chocolate makers have vast quantities of chocolates even so-called truffles – available for distribution for the holidays. It turned out that some started making their Christmas chocolates as early as March and they, of course, had to use preservatives. It gives a wholly different meaning to the word 'fresh.'

On Christmas Eve there seemed to be an endless queue snaking out well into the street. Having no time to eat we forgot about lunch when Patricia Payne walked in at 3.00 p.m. bearing a tray of spicy Indian food. Never has chicken tandoori tasted so good.

What the Indian spice aromas did to that day's truffles we'll never know!

Vodka Lime

Yield: 30 truffles

Ingredients

US Recipe	UK Recipe
13 ½ oz white chocolate	13 ½ oz white chocolate
4 oz heavy cream	8 oz double cream
4 oz clarified butter	4 oz unsalted butter
3 tsp grated lime zest	3 tsp grated lime zest
3 ½ tbsp lime/ lemon Juice	3 ½ tbsp lime/lemon juice
3 tbsp Vodka	3 tbsp Vodka

Coating
Tempered white chocolate
Grated lemon peel for decoration

Directions
Grate the zest of two limes. Squeeze the juice of the limes, make up to 3 ½ tbsp with lemon juice and reserve. In a small pan boil cream to reduce it to 2 Oz's. Add butter and lime zest and bring to a boil. Pour over broken pieces of chocolate in a bowl, cover and let rest for 2 minutes. Stir gently to blend. If all chocolate has not melted, heat in microwave for 15 seconds stirring gently each time until fully blended. Cool 5 minutes.

Carefully add juice followed by vodka one tbsp at a time mixing well with each addition. Refrigerate till firm. Scoop into balls and freeze in air tight container. Dip frozen balls in tempered white chocolate and sprinkle a little grated peel on each before coating has completely set.

~~~~~

Dee O'Hara, the legendary nurse of the original seven astronauts, who later became Joan's close friend, was the inspiration for the Vodka Lime Truffle. Joan first met her when after a particularly traumatic day on the job she asked for a vodka lime.

Later, we also noticed that a tart lemony taste was popular even with our very dark chocolate addicts. Intriguing how the sense of smell and taste make partners of apparent contradictions. For instance, although Cointreau was the outright winner of our white chocolate truffles, Joan found them a bit mild for her taste. This is how she started experimenting with a Vodka Lime concoction.

Tia Maria Truffle

Yetta was a somewhat shy Danish lady who 'found' us and dropped in for a chat from time to time. One day she brought in her newly-born child and surprised Geoffrey by saying his name was Hassan, not too unlike Geoffrey's own surname. It transpired that her husband was Omar Kassem, a successful entrepreneur with close links to the former Egyptian Royal Family. Omar was educated at Tonbridge in Kent and spoke impeccable English.

The Tia Maria recipe was created in Joan's mind by the marriage of these two events. Tia Maria has great flavor all of itself but in a truffle was somewhat bland. Omar Kassem's Egyptian heritage inspired her to produce a Tia Maria white chocolate truffle that would conjure childhood memories of *mahalabaya*, the favorite Egyptian dessert of rice pudding sprinkled with cinnamon. Would this work? The answer came next time Omar walked into the shop. He soon made a point of appearing almost every evening on his way home when Joan indulged his chocoholic fancies much to Yetta's frustration. One Sunday Geoffrey was invited for brunch to enjoy Beluga caviar and champagne along with a tour of his impressive paintings.

Yield: 30 truffles

Ingredients

US Recipe	**UK Recipe**
13 ½ oz white chocolate	8 oz white chocolate
2 oz heavy whipping cream	6 oz double cream
3 oz clarified butter	3 oz unsalted butter
⅓ tsp Nescafé	⅓ tsp Nescafé
0.1 tsp cinnamon or taste	0.1 tsp cinnamon or to taste
1 tbsp Cognac	1 tbsp Cognac
2 tbsp Tia Maria	2 tbsp Tia Maria

Coating
Tempered white chocolate
Melted dark chocolate for decoration

Directions

Boil cream in small pan to reduce to 1 oz. Add butter, Nescafé and cinnamon over low heat. When it starts to boil, turn off heat, stir to blend.

Add all chocolate in small broken pieces making sure cream mixture covers chocolate. Allow to sit for 2-3 minutes. Stir gently just to melt chocolate and blend.

Allow to cool uncovered stirring occasionally. When at room temperature, add cognac and Tia Maria one tbsp at a time making sure it blends well. Cool in refrigerator until it sets hard, preferably overnight. This is most important as the mix will otherwise be sticky and hard to handle. Scoop, roll lightly in your hands and return balls to refrigerator.

Freeze in an air-tight container. Dip frozen balls in tempered white chocolate. After the coating sets, pipe a dark chocolate TM decoration on each truffle.

~~~~~

At about that time, a public relations firm was handling the promotion of the Tia Maria liqueur and asked us to make a special truffle for a promotional launch. This was just the kind of challenge we enjoyed. Royal Worcester produced a 5" wide white gold-rimmed fine bone China bowl with a specially stamped Tia Maria label which we filled with our limited-edition designer Tia Maria chocolate truffles. We wrapped the dishes in cellophane and tied a rich brown ribbon around them. They were then placed in a square custom-made brown gold-rimmed box. A cream flat ribbon secured this box which in turn was placed in a made-to-order corrugated carton for shipping.

As always on these occasions we heaved a vast sigh of relief once they were safely delivered.

Designer Truffles
Expanding Our Line

*H*aving made chocolate truffles for two years we thought it might be time to actually learn how to make them. At the end of a five-month stint at Ames running yet another bed-rest study, Joan took a week's leave to attend a short course in Continental Chocolates run by Richardson Researches in Hayward, California. Amongst the course members were a Los Altos policeman looking for a change of career, a Japanese who stayed up studying until 2.00 a.m., representatives from chocolate companies in Venezuela, Mexico and the USA, along with Adrienne Welch, author of *Sweet Seduction* and maker of truffles exclusively for Bloomingdale's. Joan learned how to identify good and bad cocoa-beans, how to differentiate raw chocolate from around the world, the manufacturing process of *couverture* and the differences between machine and hand-made chocolates. After a written examination she was awarded a certificate. The course was informative but changed very little in the way we made our truffles.

Designer Truffles

The recipes for truffles in this book are not the only ones we made for GEOFFROI. Others not listed here were dark chocolate Bourbon Truffles, a Ginger Truffle and the Benedictine Truffles we made for a special promotional Christmas gift for the Benedictine liqueur. These were variants of the Grand Marnier dark chocolate coated truffle. You can see how you can play around with the basic recipes and adapt them to whatever is your favorite spirit or flavor.

We made an excellent Mint Truffle flavored with Crème de Menthe. But we soon realized that although it was a huge success it could not be included with other truffles in a box without overwhelming the rest with mint flavor. It was even hard to store Mint Truffles in the refrigerator or the freezer.

We made a Kahlua Truffle, a Raspberry Chambord for some customers and a sensational Green Chartreuse white chocolate truffle with chopped pistachio decoration for another special order. As you can tell a great deal of our business was customized, designer truffles for special customers. By making small batches of hand-made truffles we were able to respond and it was always fun to come up with something new.

Cherry Kirsch was so popular that it was a natural progression to adapt the recipe. Something flavored with coconut was often suggested. Joan's personal dislike of coconut delayed its creation but she finally succumbed.

Malibu

This recipe has more chocolate to cream than its relative, the Cherry Kirsch, to accommodate the larger amount of liquid (liqueurs) needed to provide adequate flavor.

Yield 36 truffles

Ingredients

US recipe	**UK recipe**
8 oz heavy cream	6 oz double cream
18 oz milk chocolate	3 oz milk chocolate
½ cup candied pineapple	½ cup candied pineapple
3 tbsp Malibu liqueur	3 tbsp Malibu
1 tbsp white Rum	1 tbsp white Rum
NB. Boil cream to reduce to 4ozs	

Coating
Chopped toasted coconut

Directions
Prepare candied pineapple by soaking overnight with the 1 tbsp white rum. This facilitates chopping in the food processor. Chop pineapple mixture in food processor and store refrigerated until used.

Heat the cream to simmering. Pour the hot cream over the broken pieces of chocolate. Microwave on medium in 15 second installments taking care not to scorch, letting the mixture rest for two minutes and stirring after each cycle, until smooth.

Add pineapple and Malibu and blend. Refrigerate covered overnight.

Scoop and shape into balls. Roll in toasted coconut just before serving. Best eaten fresh or store frozen.

Cranberry Truffles

Yield 24 truffles

Ingredients

2/3 cup fresh cranberries, washed
½ cup sugar
¼ cup water
2 tbsp water

8 oz semisweet chocolate
6 oz clarified butter
2 tbsp gin

Coating
Tempered dark chocolate
Unsweetened cocoa

Directions
Prick cranberries all over with a fork. Combine ½ cup sugar with ¼ cup water in medium saucepan over low heat and cook until sugar dissolves, shaking pan occasionally. Increase heat and cook until candy thermometer reaches 238°F (soft-ball stage). Add cranberries and stir until mixture is thick, sticky and thermometer registers 250°F (hard-ball stage). Let cool 1 hour, stirring occasionally. Remove cranberries from syrup and set aside.

Add 2 tbsp water to cranberry syrup. Place syrup over low heat and simmer until it thickens, swirling pan occasionally. Set aside.

Melt butter and chocolate in microwave by heating for 30 secs, stirring to mix and heating a further 30 seconds. Stir well until blended. Add cranberries, gin and 2 teaspoons of the cranberry syrup. Refrigerate until firm.

Scoop out balls and roll in tempered chocolate in palm of hand. Drop ball on flat sieve and roll with fork. When coating is almost set roll in unsweetened cocoa. Bitterness of cocoa complements sweetness of truffle. Store in tight-fitting lid box and refrigerate for no more than a week.

~~~~~

A well-dressed bejeweled Mediterranean lady came in one afternoon clutching what was obviously an expensive chocolate assortment – not a GEOFFROI box. The cellophane wrapping had been pierced and she proceeded to explain that there was one chocolate missing – probably tasted when she received the gift. Would we oblige by filling the gap and rewrapping the box? At no charge, we gave this thick-skinned person a dipped apricot but declined to rewrap the box. In all likelihood she was a customer's friend and we were glad not to see her again.

Another customer once complained that a chocolate was missing from our ½ lb circular presentation box. We could only conclude that the ribboned bow had been somehow slipped off and then replaced as Joan and I personally packaged each box! Again there was no charge, but we marveled at human ingenuity.

The Dubliner

This was inspired from our popular Chocolate Torte and named after the famous bar in Washington DC. It has become our most popular dark chocolate truffle, next to rum of course.

The Dubliner

Yield: 36 truffles

Ingredients

½ cup raisins
3 tbsp Rose's Irish Whiskey
10 oz semi-sweet dark chocolate
8 oz heavy cream
10 oz bitter-sweet dark chocolate
2 tbsp clarified butter

Directions

Add whiskey to raisins, cover and soak overnight. Cut chocolate into ½ inch pieces in a bowl and melt in microwave for 1 minute. Stir to mix. It should be softened but not completely melted. Boil cream I to reduce to 6 Oz's. Add butter, stir and pour over chocolate. Allow to sit covered for about 2 minutes. Stir gently until chocolate is completely melted.

Blend in raisins and whiskey. Stir gently once or twice to mix raisins uniformly until cool. Refrigerate until set giving the mixture a periodic gentle stir so raisins do not settle in the bottom of the bowl.

Scoop balls of truffle mixture onto parchment or waxed paper. Roll into balls and store in tightly sealed foil pans in freezer.

Dip in tempered dark chocolate and immediately transfer to rack with ¼ inch wire mesh. Using a tooth-pick, roll truffles across mesh as chocolate sets to produce traditional pointed markings. Store in an airtight container in the refrigerator or freezer.

~~~~~

Most of our clientele tended to appear on Saturday afternoons. These regulars would walk in as if on a social visit. Couples at work during the week came to relax, be introduced to neighbors, help fill in *The Times* crossword and generally partake of a salon atmosphere. A vicar had attended two funerals and his home was inundated with flowers. Would we mind if he brought some in? A house decorator would have his wife stand outside with their Alsatian dog flaring his nostrils whilst goodies were piled up inside.

Given the minute size of our operation, we proved versatile. For two years, we supplied 100 gift boxes of chocolates for the *Connoisseur* magazine's Antiques Fair charity champagne preview at Grosvenor House in Piccadilly. Delivering the beribboned boxes safely and somehow ensuring the product remained cool on a hot summer's day was part of the challenge. Auto World Wine Club offered their members the opportunity to buy Benedictine liqueur or Gaston De Lagrange Cognac with complimentary GEOFFROI chocolates. Roy Lack, one of many customers who became a friend, repeatedly invited us to exhibit our chocolates at Aquascutum in Regent Street when specially invited Japanese guests were asked to come and shop after hours. Indirectly, too, some of our chocolates proved popular in Royal circles at Christmas.

Maurice and Judy Levitt from nearby Vicars Moor Lane were regular and cheerful customers. Maurice, a Midlands textile manufacturer, was a sharp observer of human nature with a seemingly inexhaustible supply of jokes which he continues to ply by email.

Carole Hand and family were always most encouraging and reassuring often inviting me home for a welcome cooked meal when Joan was away. The village folk – and the list is long – were all truly supportive.

Diet Truffles

*W*e were often asked for a lower calorie rum truffle. That got us started on developing some sugar-free truffles that diabetics could enjoy. It was not easy because bitter chocolate (without sugar) is temperamental – difficult to work with and may curdle. We were lucky in using Caxton's 1196, a delicious bitter chocolate. We have made them with Baker's cooking chocolate but the truffles are not nearly as good.

Diet Rum Truffle

These diet rum truffles were essentially indistinguishable from the real thing.

Yield: 24 truffles

Ingredients

US recipe	UK recipe
8 oz unsweetened dark Chocolate	8 oz unsweetened dark chocolate
8 oz heavy cream	8 oz double cream
3 packets saccharin	(1.6mg) or about 4 packets Splenda
2 tbsp dark rum	2 tbsp dark rum

Directions
Break up chocolate into small pieces.

Bring cream to a boil. For US recipe boil cream down to 6 oz). Add sweetener. Taste to make sure it is sweet enough.

Pour hot cream over chocolate. Cover and let sit 3 minutes. Gently stir to melt. Allow to cool and thicken at room temperature to avoid curdling.

Add rum to cool mixture and blend. Transfer to refrigerator until set.

~~~~~

Early in January Geoffrey picked up the telephone and heard a lady say that our diet truffles had a green coating! Taken aback he suggested that these might perhaps be pistachio nuts, but was assured they were not. On further delving we were told that the box had been wrapped in tinsel and put under the warm Christmas tree lights. The consequences were disastrous.

These fresh cream hand-made chocolates are best kept in a cool dry place and eaten within 10-14 days.

Geoffroi & Co.   *01-360-8289*
65 Station Road   •   London N21 3NB

The GEOFFROI freshness and storage warning label

Each and every box had a warning label inside saying the truffles needed to be kept cool and eaten within 10-14 days.

Obviously, the final recipient was unaware of this advice. Happily, this was our only 'complaint' in the history of GEOFFROI and one that was amicably resolved.

We made diet versions of some other truffle recipes to offer variety to our diabetic customers. Walnut cognac and an apricot truffle were much in demand.

Walnut Cognac Truffle

We made several diet versions of our regular truffles so that our diabetics or dieting customers would not feel shortchanged. As with the rum truffles, these were indistinguishable.

Walnut Cognac and Amaretto Truffles. The Nut Collection

Yield 24 truffles

Ingredient

(Regular)	**(Diet)**
8 oz bitter-sweet dark Chocolate	8 oz unsweetened dark chocolate
8 oz heavy cream	8 oz heavy cream
2 tbsp Cognac	2 tbsp Cognac
	2 packets saccharin or 3-4 packets
	Splenda walnut halves walnut halves

Directions

Cut chocolate in ½" pieces and melt in microwave 15 secs.

Boil cream to reduce to 6 ozs. Add sweetener and stir till blended. Pour hot cream over chocolate, cover for 2 minutes then gently blend till smooth. Mix in cognac. Cool mixture completely and refrigerate overnight.

Form into small balls. These can now be frozen in a tightly covered container.

Regular Walnut Truffles: Coat frozen balls in dark tempered chocolate. Before completely set place a walnut half on either side of coated truffle and squeeze gently.

Diet Walnut Truffle: These truffles are uncoated. When ready to serve, bring dietetic chocolate balls almost to room temperature. With clean hands, press two walnut halves on either side of each small chocolate ganache ball. Gently squeeze walnuts together until chocolate truffle mixture reaches the walnut edges.

~~~~~

A young well-spoken man came in one day with a plain plastic bag containing what looked like tobacco. Could we produce chocolate bars with tobacco in them for sale through newsagents where children buy their sweets?

We were already making Happy Birthday and Happy New Year molded bars wrapped in specially initialed boxes so we should perhaps not have been quite so surprised. Joan was anything but gullible and one sniff at the bag soon established that the 'tobacco' was another form of 'grass.' Shades of Alice B. Toklas pot brownies sent shivers up her spine. Visions of headlines like "NASA pharmacologist provides chocolate highs" flashed through her mind – hardly the kind of publicity we would undoubtedly court. We suggested that he contact Caxton's as we were not in the wholesale chocolate bar manufacturing business and heaved a sigh of relief. We never saw him again.

Apricot Truffle

Yield: 24 truffles

Ingredients

(Regular)	**(Diet)**
8 oz heavy cream	8 oz heavy cream
9 oz bittersweet dark chocolate	9 oz unsweetened dark chocolate
2 tbsp Bols Advocaat	2 tbsp Cognac
¼ cup finely-chopped dried apricots	¼ cup finely chopped dried apricots
	Splenda or Saccharin to taste

Directions
Chop enough dried apricots to end up with ¼ cup of packed apricots. Add Bols Advocaat or Cognac and soak overnight covered to soften.

Chop chocolate in 16 oz glass oven-proof cup. In small heavy pan boil cream until reduced to 6 ozs.

Add cream to chopped chocolate pieces slowly mixing to blend. Heat in microwave if needed, 5 secs at a time, mixing between each until completely melted.

Add apricot mixture to cooled cream and chocolate *ganache*. Whip with electric mixer on high 2-3 minutes. Cool and scoop. Roll balls in finely ground toasted almonds.

Best eaten fresh.

~~~~~

The Times (16 March 1985) had photographs of Joan molding a big chocolate Easter bunny and then coloring an orange and green carrot with white teeth! News of the sugar-free truffle had gone the rounds and she was quoted as saying, "Astronauts have to be extremely careful about what they eat, because weightlessness can affect hormone regulation.

At the moment astronauts have to be careful even drinking coffee, and we think vanilla in chocolate could also upset their metabolism. However, as the shuttle program gets under way, diets in space will become increasingly liberal, and certainly the sugar-free truffle is ideal for anyone with a sweet tooth whose sugar intake is limited." Sugar-free truffles were not cholesterol free and would not help shed much weight.

All this media coverage resulted in bags of mail. Chocolatiers from Ireland, the United States and Trinidad trekked out to see us and exchange ideas. But the chocolate industry is notoriously secretive and guards its hard-earned knowledge. Understandably, there was special interest in our sugar-free truffles and the precise content of the sugar substitute. One censored letter arrived from Broadmoor maximum security psychiatric hospital for the criminally insane in Crowthorne, Berkshire, where the patient, a self-declared fitness fiend, did not like sugar. Would we please send a brochure as it was impossible for him to come and visit the shop. This gave us cause for reflection but, as with all other correspondence, his letter was promptly answered.

Roger Harvey, then a tall young trombonist, had a liking for chocolate and would bring his sons in with him by way of a treat. One was a Manchester United fan and so found instant favor with me! Roger has been the principal trombone of the Hallé Orchestra and a Director of London Brass. One day he gave me a ride into town and soon got caught up in London Traffic thereby almost missing a rehearsal at the Albert Hall.

Fruits, Mints & Ice Cream Sauce

$\mathcal{A}$long with truffles we played around with dipping various nuts, dried or candied fruit in chocolate. Candied apricots, pear, ginger or orange peel dipped in dark chocolate could be found in many chocolate shops. Though our bitter orange candied peel chocolate sticks and our crystallized ginger dipped in dark chocolate became winners, pears and apricots seemed overly sweet. We experimented with dried fruit instead. The tartness of a juicy dried apricot is balanced by the sweetness of the chocolate. Most dried apricots tend to be on the dry side and care is needed in selecting the right fruit that is still plump. For fun we also tried dipping the apricots in white chocolate. Soon we stopped dipping any in dark chocolate. Our white chocolate dipped apricots have remained an all-time winner.

White Chocolate Dried Apricots

Apricots in White Chocolate & Orange Sticks in Dark Chocolate

Starting with the right ingredients they are easy to make because tempering white chocolate – the process of melting and cooling the chocolate back to body temperature while stirring with a quality tempered piece of chocolate to 'seed' the melted mixture – is easier than tempering dark chocolate.

Once at the right temperature, when it no longer feels warm on the lip or the inside part of the wrist, dip each apricot quickly and place on a sheet of waxed paper on a cool counter until set. The coolness of the counter helps and marble is ideal. If the chocolate is well-tempered it will set very quickly.

Transfer and store the dipped apricots in a tightly closing plastic container in a cool place (no refrigeration needed).

Chocolate will pick up odors and flavors from anything around so never store chocolate in an open container in the refrigerator. Tin containers may also impart a strange taste to these apricots unless well lined with wax paper.

~~~~~

Sports devotees from all walks of life love their chocolates and would regularly find their way to our shop. Jim Farbon, our neighbor, had put out the good word. The Trent Park Trotters, his group of local joggers, would make up for the calories they had burned by stopping by after a run. Our white chocolate-dipped dried apricots were a favorite with his marathoners. Owen Sela, a thriller novelist, was among a new set of friends which included many New Zealanders. To this day, for instance, Karen and Kevin Underwood send us Christmas cards and photographs of their boys.

White Chocolate Dried Bananas

Elizabeth Dare, who ran a trendy Dried Fruit and Nut health food shop in the Bond Street tube station, bought some of our macadamia nuts and then asked if we could dip dried bananas from Indonesia into tempered white chocolate. We had to prize the dried bananas apart before dipping but it was useful business particularly when we were quiet.

For a while all went well. Orders doubled. Instead of using one hand Geoffrey used two. With a little dexterity four banana slices could be hand-dipped at the same time!

Then disaster struck when Irish nationalists exploded a bomb on the Bond Street underground. Overnight, the health food shop went out of business. Nevertheless, we were paid and the white chocolate bananas have remained as popular as the apricots.

~~~~~

Macadamia nuts from Namibia were among some of the gourmet products on our shelves. Hawaiian macadamias were sold at an exorbitant price at Fortnum and Mason's but few then knew what they tasted like, not even the barman at Claridge's Hotel. Mrs Dare then came to visit with a friend and very kindly arranged for us to meet Lady Elisabeth Anson, a cousin of the Queen, who, with the help of debutantes, ran Party Planners. One evening over sherry and with a flower arranger fussing around we explained the scale of our little enterprise with particular emphasis on the truffles. Foolishly, in retrospect, we also mentioned the *bonbonnières* or little lace bags – hand-sewn by Joan on her regular transatlantic flights – tied with a pink ribbon and filled with delicately fine French sugared almonds often given out to guests at confirmations or weddings. An order for 100 followed. These were destined for a lavish Jordanian wedding reception at Claridge's where the bag inside a small woven silver basket bought from Asprey's was hung on a tree with twinkling lights in the foyer. Disenchantment set in when we were asked what the price of each bag would be if we put in one less almond.

Mint Squares

These were small squares of a dark chocolate fudgy centre coated in dark chocolate. This recipe was labor intensive to make by hand because each little square was individually coated.

Yield 50 mints

Ingredients

18 oz dark bittersweet chocolate
14 oz can sweetened condensed milk Dash of salt
¼ tsp peppermint oil*

Coating
Dark bittersweet chocolate

Directions
Melt chocolate with condensed milk in microwave for 30 seconds. Gently stir to blend before reheating for another 15 -30 sec if necessary. Add salt and the peppermint oil.

Spread mixture evenly into wax-paper-lined ½ inch deep baking pan. Chill 2-3 hours until firm. Cover with foil to prevent contamination of other food in refrigerator with mint odor.

Turn onto cutting board. Peel off paper. Cut into ½ inch squares. Cover with foil again until coating. Coat each square with tempered dark chocolate coating.

Store in tightly closed container in cool place or refrigerated. NB. These mints are stable for at least two weeks. * To avoid lumping or curdling, it is important to use peppermint oil and not essence or extract even if it says alcohol-free on the label. The slightest drop of moisture will curdle the chocolate.

~~~~~

An estate agent came in at regular intervals for a large oval personalized green and gold box of these mint squares. He would request we remove the GEOFFROI label on the inside of the box lid!

We had many an uncommon request. One order consisted of a hollow chocolate Christmas bear to contain a ring. Another more risky one involved hiding two special earrings inside truffles in a box of identical Cointreau truffles. We were concerned. He was adamant that he would remember which were the 'jeweled truffles.'

Mint Wafers

These are thin crunchy chocolate wafers. Though fragile they are stable. They make an imaginative and elegant dinner present.

Chocolate Mint Wafers

Ingredients

1 lb bittersweet dark chocolate
1 tbsp sugar Peppermint oil*

Directions

Break up, melt and temper chocolate as described previously. Blend in oil to taste.

When coming close to being tempered stir in sugar and drop a dessert spoon at a time on cellophane paper which imparts a beautiful sheen to one side of the wafer. You may have to ease it off the spoon with another spoon. As the mixture thickens it can become hard to work with and may need very slight rewarming. Works best if made in small batches. Store mint wafers in cool place in a tightly closing tin.

 * It is important to use Peppermint oil rather than extract or essence to avoid curdling.

~~~~~

When summer hit we were asked whether we could make chocolate sauce for ice cream. Those of our customers who had visited or spent time in the USA had experienced chocolate sundaes. So the research team of one went to work. Chocolate sundaes are an American invention so we had no idea how well the sauces would do. Also standard recipes available contained corn syrup which was not available in the UK.

 We found that liquid glucose found at the chemist's seemed to work as well. However, neither corn syrup nor liquid glucose is considered particularly healthy. So we experimented with honey which works as long as it is the kind made by bees rather than the human imitation. Oh, yes, much of commercial honey is man-made if you read the fine print. The aroma in natural honey that comes from the different herbs the bees visit also imparts a faintly unusual flavor to the sauce and gives the chocolate an interesting twist. You can experiment with different honeys as long as they are very thick.

Chocolate Fudge Sauce

Our customers said "Forget the Ice Cream." They ate the Chocolate Fudge Sauce with a spoon straight from the jar!

Yield four 8 oz jars. It can be doubled, for a larger batch.

Ingredients

1 cup sugar
1 cup dark brown sugar
4 tbsp Greek honey
1 cup heavy cream
8 tbsp (1 stick) salted butter
6 ozs dark chocolate broken up (72% cocoa liquor)

Directions
Put sugars, honey, cream and butter in a 2-quart saucepan (it bubbles and may overflow in a smaller pan). Heat mixture stirring occasionally to blend and bring to a boil. Boil 3 to 5 minutes. The longer it cooks, the chewier the sauce will be.

 Remove from heat and allow to stand for 5 minutes.

Add the chocolate stirring continuously until melted and completely blended in. Pour into sterilized jars and seal. This thick sauce requires heating to serve. If it becomes too thick or grainy when reheated, add a tablespoon of cream until the texture is properly thick and smooth.

~~~~~

Butter Caramel Sauce

Having experienced the Fudge Sauce, visitors soon asked, "What next?" Butter Caramel Sauce seemed the obvious partner.

Yield Nine 8 oz jars

Ingredients

3 cups white sugar
3 cups brown sugar
2 sticks (8 ozs) salted butter
1 cup heavy cream
6 tbsp Greek honey

Directions
Put sugars, honey, cream and butter in a large pan to avoid overflow when it boils.

Heat mixture over low heat stirring occasionally to blend. Remove spoon and raise heat to a boil.

Boil 8 minutes reducing heat to control bubbling. Turn heat off. Remove from heat and allow to stand 8 minutes. Stir well to blend for another 10-15 minutes. Cool slightly, pour into sterilized jars and seal.

~~~~~

The GEOFFROI Suite of Cakes

"Strength is the capacity to break a chocolate bar into four pieces with your bare hands – then eat just one of the pieces."

---Judith Viorst, Washington DC.

We were regularly asked to bake conventional chocolate cakes, but this was not the path we chose to follow. Instead, this rich torte soon became a talking point in the village and customers could either buy it whole or by the slice. We always warned that a little bit went a long way and would sink you for a couple of hours. This was also a popular desert at dinner parties. Olivia commented to Joan that "the cake could not be any fresher – just like your husband!"

Chocolate Decadence Torte

GEOFFROI *Chocolate Decadence Torte*

Ingredients

½ cup raisins
½ cup brandy
14 ozs semisweet dark chocolate
¼ cup water
½ lb unsalted butter
6 jumbo eggs, separated
1 tbsp sugar
9 tbsp cake flour

1 cup ground pecans Pinch of salt

Ganache Icing
8 ozs semisweet dark chocolate
8 ozs heavy cream

Directions
Soak raisins in brandy overnight.

Use two buttered 6" spring-form pans or one 8" pan for a taller cake. Butter pans well and line with wax paper. Preheat oven to 350°.

In a double boiler over hot not boiling water, melt together the chocolate and water. Stir until smooth.

Stir in butter in small pieces, keeping the mixture smooth. Remove from heat. In a separate bowl, beat egg yolks and sugar until creamy and thick. Stir into the chocolate mixture. Add flour one tablespoon at a time. Add raisins and brandy followed by pecans. Mix together gently but thoroughly.

Beat egg whites with salt until stiff, but not dry. Fold by thirds into the batter gently.

Pour batter into prepared pans and bake in preheated oven for 30 minutes. It will seem moist in the center, but the sides will start to shrink from the pan edges.

Allow to cool in the pan for 10 minutes. Remove rim of spring-form pan and paper lining and finish cooling. After complete cooling place a round cardboard cake base edged with parchment paper strips onto cake and turn over. Meanwhile make the icing.

Melt chocolate and cream together over double boiler stirring to keep smooth. Icing should be thick but pourable. If too thin cool over ice cubes.

Pour *ganache* icing over the top and sides of cake, smoothing with a spatula. Remove wax paper strips. Allow to set. Store in the refrigerator till ready to serve.

The cake is elegant as it is but you may wish to add your own individual decorative touch. Excellent served on a plate decorated with raspberry coulis.

Each cake serves 8-10 chocoholics. The cake is very rich and thin slices are quite adequate.

Instead of two round pans you may use a 12" square pan or similar size that will serve about 20 square pieces.

NB: The recipe can be readily halved.

Wrapped tightly in aluminum foil, the cakes will keep perfectly well in the freezer.

~~~~~

On one of Joan's many trips away from the shop, David Cole, a customer famous in Smithfield's 800-year-old wholesale Meat Market for running out and blowing the bugle whenever the parking Meter Maids were on the prowl, repeatedly asked if I could make him one of our truffle cakes except that he wanted it made with white instead of the usual dark chocolate. White chocolate is of such a different consistency and formulation that I had serious doubts about whether the same recipe would set merely by replacing dark with white chocolate. After discussing the issue with Joan we came to the conclusion that this had potential, but needed further research before getting it right enough to sell. Since then Geoffrey brought up the subject a few times and we finally decided to test it out. The following recipes of our white chocolate truffle cake are variations on our chocolate truffles. Enjoy them!

White Chocolate Truffle Cake

Ingredients

14 oz white chocolate
¼ cup water
½ lb (250g) unsalted butter
6 large eggs
4 tbsp sugar
6 tbsp Bisquick or other fine cake flour
1 cup almonds ground fine*
¾ cup dried apricots ground fine
½ cup vodka

Directions
Soak ground apricots in vodka overnight. Preheat oven to 350°. Butter two 6" pans (or one 6" and one 8") and line with wax paper.

Bring butter to room temperature. Melt chocolate and water stirring gently till smooth add butter and mix gently. Separate eggs. Beat egg yolks with 2 tbsp sugar till frothy and increased in volume. Add to chocolate and mix.

Add apricots in vodka, almonds and cake flour. Stir well. Beat egg whites till stiff with pinch of salt. Fold into cake mixture gently in three additions.

Pour into prepared pans and bake for 35 minutes. Cool.

NB. For variety, try walnuts instead of almonds; use only 2 tbsp sugar if you want to reduce the sugar content.

Dark Chocolate Ganache Icing
Drizzle a bit of Amaretto before icing with dark chocolate. Or try Irish coffee version or vodka lime described below.

Ice the cake with dark chocolate to give it greater chocolate flavor. Use the same recipe as for the dark chocolate truffle cake.

8oz heavy cream
8oz bittersweet chocolate

Heat cream almost to boiling. Break chocolate into small pieces in a small bowl and heat in microwave for 1 minute. Stir gently – it should be soft but not melted. Add warm cream and allow to sit for a few minutes. Stir gently till blended and smooth. Cover cold cake with melted chocolate icing. Allow to cool to room temperature and refrigerate.

Topping
Frozen raspberries
½ cup sugar or syrup
½ cup low sugar raspberry fruit spread (or jelly)
Strip of fresh orange peel

Directions
Drain raspberry juice into a small pan, add sugar and orange peel. Bring to boil till reduced in volume to half. Cool. Add raspberry fruit spread and stir to blend. Add raspberries and fold in gently. Store refrigerated till used.
Slice cake into thin wedges and pour a small amount of raspberry topping to one side of slice.

Variations
An Irish Coffee variation (see truffle) would be interesting. Omit apricots, retain skinless almonds ground finely*, use coffee to flavor as for truffle and blend in Irish Whiskey into mixture before folding in egg whites. Ice with white chocolate/cream icing, decorate with dark chocolate-covered coffee beans.

Vodka Lime variation (see truffle). Omit apricots. Retain almonds*. Grate 1 lime peel and boil till reduced to pulp. Cool. Add ½ cup vodka and allow to macerate overnight. Ice with white chocolate/cream icing. Decorate with candied lemon slivers and serve with lemon curd on the side or place a slice on a bed of lemon curd.

Cherry Kirsch variation (see truffle). Use ½ cup ground glace cherries. Add ½ cup Kirsch. Omit apricots. Retain almonds*. Ice with dark chocolate. Serve with brandied cherries. *Found in specialty stores as almond meal.

As years went by chocolate connoisseurs became more health conscious. First, it was the sugar so we reduced the sugar content which actually improved the taste of the cake. Then there were those who were allergic to nuts and those who worried about the carbohydrate content in general. Chocolate started to be vilified as being harmful until it was shown to be rich in antioxidants and therefore good for one's health. So we decided to try our hand at a flourless version of our truffle cake to provide an alternative dark chocolate truffle cake line.

Geoffroi's Flourless Chocolate Truffle Cake

Ingredients
12 oz bittersweet or semisweet chocolate
12 tbsp unsalted butter at room temperature
8 jumbo eggs separated
2/3 cup sugar
1.5 oz raisins
2 tbsp cognac

Directions
Soak raisins in cognac overnight.

Preheat oven to 350°. Butter two 6" spring-form pans; line with buttered wax paper.

Melt chocolate in microwave oven for 1 minute. Stir gently till smooth. Add butter cut in cubes and beat another 30 seconds. Stir till smooth. Whip egg yolks with sugar until light in color and tripled in volume. Add chocolate to yolk mixture and mix till blended. Add soaked raisins.

Whip egg whites with a pinch of salt till stiff meringue. Fold meringue into chocolate mixture in three additions blending lightly. Bake about 45 minutes. *Center will still be soft but cake will pull away from rim. Cool in pan.* Remove pan and paper. Sprinkle with powdered sugar or ice with dark chocolate *ganache.*

Ganache icing
8 oz semisweet or bittersweet chocolate
8 oz heavy cream

Bring cream almost to boil. Break chocolate into small pieces in small bowl and heat in microwave for 1 minute. Add hot cream and allow to sit until chocolate appears melted. Mix gently until smooth.

Raspberry Coulis
5 cups raspberries rinsed
¼ cup sugar
Fresh mint

In a food processor or blender, whirl one quart raspberries until smooth. Rub purée through a fine strainer into a bowl; discard seeds. Stir sugar into raspberry purée; taste.

Spoon raspberry *coulis* onto plates. Cut torte into wedges. Arrange a wedge on sauce on each plate. Scatter remaining raspberries over desserts and garnish with mint sprigs.

Coconut Variation
Sprinkle toasted coconut over the top. This is an excellent variation.

~~~~~

Chocolate Truffle Bombe

Another variation on our truffle-based desserts – a delicious dessert for a buffet reception – was the Truffle Bombe. Any of our cream-based truffle recipes could lend themselves to this adaptation though we tended to use a Rum Truffle or a Grand Marnier base.

The GEOFFROI Truffle Bombe with Marrons Glaces

Line with cling-film a small deep bowl or any suitable container mould of your choosing.

Prepare chocolate truffle mixture and pour into lined container. Refrigerate until set, about 24 hours. Invert onto flat serving tray or dish lined with a paper doily.

Meanwhile whip heavy whipping cream until stiff and ice the Truffle Bombe generously with the cream to cover **completely**. Decorate with truffles or *marrons glacés* and chocolate leaves.

To make chocolate leaves spread some tempered dark chocolate on the lower side of clean leaves. Holly or rose leaves do best. Allow to set completely and gently peel off the leaf. They are easy to make and very decorative – I have also decorated the Truffle Bombe with fresh flowers for a wedding.

Serve with butter knives and small vanilla wafers or dainty tea biscuits.

For a more elegant version of the Bombe that shows how much you care, serve with *Tuiles*. *Tuiles* is French for tiles. It is a special occasion biscuit to serve with something delicate like this Truffle Bombe.

Tuiles

Yield 24 tuiles

Ingredients

2 large egg whites
2/3 cup sugar Pinch of salt
6 tbsp unsalted butter
2 tbsp canola oil
½ cup plain flour
½ cup finely chopped almond

Directions
Preheat oven to 350°F.

Melt butter and cool until lukewarm.

Beat the sugar, egg whites and salt with an electric beater until the sugar has dissolved and the mixture has thickened. Add butter and oil and blend well. Stir in flour and almonds.

Drop rounded teaspoons of mixture onto greased baking sheet, leaving plenty of room in between. Spread the mixture thinly into a round with a fork.

Bake for 12 minutes or until golden brown.

Remove from oven and cool for 20 seconds, then lift off and lay over a rolling pin. They will harden as they cool.

When set, put on cooling tray. Store in a tin when cold.

~~~~~

Millionaire's Row was the name given to nearby Broad Walk in Winchmore Hill where comedian Ted Ray and androgynous pop singer Boy George once lived.

A gentleman of Greek provenance who lived there came to the shop and was nonplussed about both Joan's Greek ancestry and NASA connection. Evangelos Angelakos, a shipping magnate, told Joan about his close friendship with ex-King Constantine of Greece then resident in London. Indirectly, we thought we might receive some orders but this proved wishful thinking.

ABOUT THE AUTHOR

Joan Vernikos PhD (1934-) was born to Greek parents in Alexandria, Egypt. A pharmacologist from the Univ. of London, she taught medical students at Ohio State University before being recruited by NASA in 1964. Former Director of NASA's Life Sciences (1993-2000) she is a recognized leader in the field of stress management and coping and a pioneer of space medicine. A woman of many talents, she and her husband Geoffrey Hazzan had a chocolate truffle shop, GEOFFROI, in London in the 1980s where she invented the first all white chocolate truffle in Europe. Stories of that challenge and the recipes she created are in their 2012 book 'Adventures in Chocolate' under her married name, Joan Hazzan, co-authored with her husband.

Her NASA research led to the discovery of a revolutionary link between gravity and healthy aging. Her first book in 2004, 'The G-Connection: Harness Gravity and Reverse Aging' with a forward by John Glenn is now published in five languages and received the 2009 Book Award of the International Academy of Astronautics. 'Stress Fitness for Seniors' followed in 2009. 'Sitting Kills, Moving Heals: How Simple Everyday Movement Will Prevent Pain, Illness and Early Death -- and Exercise Alone Won't'(2011) emphasizes that the key to lifelong health is more than just traditional gym exercise, but a natural lifestyle of constant, natural movement that resists the force of gravity. 'Sitting Kills, Moving Heals' won the Finalist Award in the General Health section of the 2012 Indie Excellence Awards. 'Designed to Move: The Science-backed Program to Fight Sitting Disease & Enjoy Lifelong Health' (2016) is for everyone who wants to feel healthier and stronger - at any age. Her latest, 'Stress Beyond 50: Tools & Wisdom for a Happier, Longer Life' (2018)', Recipient of numerous other awards for science and leadership, Dr. Joan is a popular motivational speaker, health coach and consultant to organizations. (www.joanvernikos.com/aboutjoan). Her mission - to stem the trend in poor health in sedentary and stressed-out America by helping people live their entire life with fun, health and vigor. In 2018 she was inducted into the International Astronautical Federation Hall of Fame.

www.ingramcontent.com/pod-product-compliance
Lightning Source LLC
Chambersburg PA
CBHW070936120626
46546CB00004B/1433